CHRISTIAN FINANCE FOR **teens**

CHRISTIAN FINANCE FOR teens

*A Simple Guide
to Financial Wisdom
for Teens and Young Adults*

CINDY KERSEY

NEW YORK

Christian Finance for Teens
A Simple Guide to Financial Wisdom for Teens and Young Adults

ISBN 978-1-61448-754-8 paperback
ISBN 978-1-61448-755-5 eBook
Library of Congress Control Number: 2013940701

Morgan James Publishing
The Entrepreneurial Publisher
5 Penn Plaza, 23rd Floor,
New York City, New York 10001
(212) 655-5470 office • (516) 908-4496 fax
www.MorganJamesPublishing.com

Cover Design by:
Rachel Lopez
www.r2cdesign.com

Interior Design by:
Bonnie Bushman
bonnie@caboodlegraphics.com

CONTENTS

INTRODUCTION

Why is it important to study finance? The simple truth is that many people learn about finances the hard way. By learning a few basic concepts of finance, you can be ready to make better decisions that affect your money and way of life. But why is it important to study *Christian* finance? Christians need to understand how important it is to be a good steward of the material items and money God has blessed them with. After all, it belongs to God anyway; we just take care of it for a while.

Did you know that the Bible has a lot to say about money? One Bible verse that comes to mind is 1 Timothy 6:10. This verse tells us that the love of money is the root of all evil. Many have misinterpreted this to mean that having money is evil. However, it's the *love* of money that is evil. We need money and there is nothing wrong with having money. The problem arises when people become greedy and cannot be satisfied with what they have. This leads to all kinds of sin.

The purpose of this book is to help students understand basic financial concepts. It is written with the hopes that the students who take this course will remember what they have learned and will take it with them as they encounter life after high school and college.

CHAPTER 1

JOBS AND CAREERS

Introduction

Since this book is about handling money, it is important to start with a chapter on jobs and careers because without a job, most people don't have money. So let's first look at earning some money and then we will move into taking care of it.

You have probably given some thought to what you might want to do with your life after high school and college. Some of you have probably given more thought to this than others. This is a big decision, and there are a lot of factors to consider. One very important factor is: will you enjoy what you do? It is extremely important to choose a career that will be rewarding to you. Think about this, the average person spends 40 or more hours per week at their job. Multiply this by 50 weeks per year (subtracting two weeks for vacation). Multiply that by 43 years and you get 89,440+ hours. That is a lot of time! Imagine if you didn't enjoy your job. Now, realistically, all jobs are going to have aspects that are not enjoyable, but you should be looking at the overall picture.

Spiritual Gifts

Jeremiah 29:11 tells us that God has a plan for us, and it is to prosper us, not hurt us. When trying to decide on a career, look at your spiritual gifts. God has blessed each and every one of us with certain gifts. If we take these gifts from God and use them to the best of our ability and for His glory, we will enjoy what we do so much more. God has a plan for our lives, and if we follow His direction we will find joy in our lives. You can find out what your spiritual gifts are by taking tests online or possibly through your school's library or guidance office. Once you find out what your most prevalent gifts are, think of careers where you would use those gifts. For example, if teaching is your gift, consider being a teacher or counselor.

Remember to never sell yourself short and think that you can't do something. The truth is—if God wants you to do something, He will equip you in every way to do it. Think of Gideon. He really didn't believe that he had the ability to do what God had chosen him to do, but God made sure that he had everything he needed. God will do the same for you.

Many people think that work is a punishment from God. In reality, God gave us work to help us, not punish us. In Genesis 2:15, God gave Adam work before he sinned. Also, in John 5:17, Jesus said, "My Father is always at His work to this very day, and I too am working." This verse reminds us that work is not a punishment because God Himself is a worker. God does not expect us to be lazy. In the book of Proverbs, much is said about the lazy person. Some of the things it says about the lazy person is that he/she will be poor (10:4), will irritate those around him (10:26), will serve someone else (12:24), will never be satisfied (13:4), will have difficult obstacles to overcome (15:19), and will be paranoid of unrealistic danger (22:13).

When we complete a difficult task, we typically feel good about ourselves. It makes us feel like we have accomplished something, and that is a good feeling. Think about a major project or research paper that you have done. When you finished it, didn't you feel good? That is, of course, if you put forth your best effort. We must remember that no matter what we do, we should always work to the best of our abilities because God expects that of us. We should remember to work for God, not men. The next time you have a project due or a test to study for, give it your best!

Jobs vs. Careers

A job is a set of tasks performed to earn money. A career is a sequence of jobs that a person goes through in his or her lifetime. Often this sequence of jobs is related. When a person moves from one related position to another, it is called a career line. For example, someone might start as a general laborer in a construction company, move on to be a supervisor or foreman, and then move on to be a general foreman. Another example is a teacher who starts out as a substitute teacher, moves on to be a teacher, and eventually becomes a principal.

Career Choice

Some very important advice for young people when considering a career is to find out everything possible about that career. It is important to understand what a typical day on the job would be like. Also consider what some of the best and worst aspects of that job would be. Talk to people who are already in that career. If at all possible, do an internship before you decide for sure to pursue a particular career. For example, suppose you are interested in becoming a doctor. Obviously you cannot do an internship as a doctor, but maybe you could intern in a hospital or at a doctor's office and observe a typical day on the job.

What would be the worst aspect of being a doctor? Possibly the long hours, the fact that they are often on call and must be prepared to give up their weekends from time to time, or perhaps the thought of telling someone that they have a terminal illness. On the other hand, what would be the best aspect of being a doctor? Perhaps the great feeling that you actually saved a life, or the fact that it's a pretty secure job, or the fact that doctors can earn a higher income than many other careers.

When making a career choice, many factors should be considered. For example, ask yourself questions such as: "Will this career require much travel?" and "Will this career give me the challenges that I need?" Also think about your strengths and your weaknesses; could your weaknesses hurt your career? Will your strengths be used in this career?

Finding a Job

There are several ways to go about finding a job. One way is to talk with friends and relatives and let them know that you are looking for a job. It is possible that they can help you because maybe they know someone who is looking to hire. This is a basic form of networking. As you get older and more experienced, you may use more sophisticated forms of networking. Another way to find a job is to contact an employment agency. These agencies match people with jobs based on their qualifications and job openings. Sometimes these agencies can be very helpful. If you choose to go through an agency, be careful of the fees that may be involved. Always ask up front if there are any fees that you will have to pay in order to get a job through the agency. Most agencies do not charge a fee to you, but to the employer.

Many people choose a do-it-yourself approach to finding a job. They read help-wanted ads in the newspaper or online. There are some important rules to follow when using this method. First of all, read the ad thoroughly. This may sound like a no-brainer, but many people just skim the ad, get excited, and then something doesn't work out quite right. Many employment agencies also advertise in the help-wanted section, so be aware of the fact that an agency—and a fee—may be involved. Always respond to the ad in the manner that is requested in the ad. For example, if the ad says to apply in person, then you need to apply in person. If that is the case, make sure you are dressed appropriately and prepared for an on-the-spot interview. If the ad says to submit a resume of your qualifications, then that is what you need to do (we will discuss how to prepare a resume in another section).

Another approach to finding a job is to fill out job applications at various businesses or online. Often when a help-wanted ad says to apply in person, there will be an additional application on hand for the applicant to fill out. Some businesses have computers in their stores that job applicants can use to fill out an application. When filling out a job application, be sure to read it thoroughly and take your time. This may sound trivial, but pay attention to the order in which the application asks for your name (first name first or last name first). If you cannot follow simple directions, the company may not want to hire you. Also, be very careful to spell correctly, use correct grammar, and write legibly. If at all possible, have someone proofread it for you. Most importantly, be honest. Do not give any false information because it may come back on you at a later time. Never say that you are experienced in something that you are not because it could put you or someone else in a dangerous situation. Be sure that you do not omit anything. If an item does not apply to you, draw a line through that space or write "N/A" (not applicable). You do not want to make it appear that you have forgotten to answer any questions.

Writing a Resume

A resume is basically a summary of your qualifications that is done in a specific format. It is often the first impression a potential employer receives, so make it good! It should be in the proper format (see example). It should always be typed neatly and legibly unless the potential employer requests a handwritten resume. It is not a bad idea to use a better quality paper than plain white computer paper. Most people can print their own resumes, but a professional printer can give your resume that extra appeal that may catch a potential employer's eye. Make sure that you use correct grammar and spelling. If possible, have someone proofread it for you.

Your resume should be brief but complete. You do not want to bore the reader with too much detail, but you do want the reader to get as much information as necessary. Some professionals will tell you that a resume should never be more than one page. Others will allow several pages if the information is important. Use your own judgment, but it doesn't hurt to look at some websites that offer free resume assistance. Trends change and these websites can keep you up-to-date on what is appropriate at any given time.

A resume should include: your contact information (name, address, telephone number, and email address), your education, your work experience, your skills, and any other information that would show your qualifications for a particular job—such as certifications. If you speak another language fluently, this should also be listed on your resume. Always include references or at least mention that you have references available. These references should be people who know you well enough to recommend you for a particular job. They should not be family members. Make sure that you ask someone permission before listing him or her as a reference. Teachers, coaches, pastors, and previous employers make good references.

A resume should not include: salary expectations (unless a potential employer has specifically asked that you include it), age, marital status, family information, handicaps, pictures, etc. Also, be very careful when listing your email address and telephone number on your resume. These items are very important, but if your email address is not very professional, consider getting a new address for employment purposes. For example, if your email address is alwayslate@aol.com, you may want to reconsider because this says something negative about you to potential employers. Also, if you give your cell phone number, remember to answer politely in case a potential employer is calling. You might want to think about what your voicemail says as well.

Sample Resume

Sandra Jenkins
901 Heron Drive
Newport News, VA 23602
757-874-8989
sanjen@aol.com

Objective: To obtain a position as an Accounting Manager

Education: University of Virginia
B.S.B.A. with concentration in Accounting, 1998

Work Experience: 2001–present
Riverside Regional Medical Center
Newport News, VA
Accounting Clerk
Duties performed:
- Reconciled monthly bank statements
- Reconciled accounts payable ledger
- Reconciled accounts receivable ledger
- Assisted Accounting Manager with month-end financial statements
- Assisted Accounting Manager with annual budgets

1998–2001
B&B Manufacturing Company
Yorktown, VA
Bookkeeper
Duties performed:
- Reconciled monthly bank statements
- Input financial data into computer
- Reconciled customer accounts

References: Available upon request

Cover Letters

A cover letter should always be sent with a resume. It is a formal business letter that allows you to communicate more personally with a potential employer. In a cover letter you can give a few more details that might be helpful for a particular job. When writing a cover letter, it also helps to know something about the company to which you are applying. Do some research by checking to see if the company has a website, and if so use the website to gain some knowledge of the company. The cover letter should convey this knowledge. A cover letter should also draw attention to an enclosed resume and specify which job you are applying for. Often businesses are advertising for more than one position at a time, so a cover letter lets the potential employer know which position you are interested in. For example, a construction company might be running ads for general laborers, office clerks, and backhoe operators at any given time. If you send in your resume without a cover letter, it could be confusing as to which of the positions you are applying for.

A cover letter should be brief and businesslike. It should always be typed unless the potential employer has asked for a handwritten copy. The cover letter should be in proper business format. Always use proper grammar and make sure everything is spelled correctly. There should be a statement in the letter that brings attention to your enclosed resume. For example, "For your convenience, I have enclosed a copy of my resume." Also make sure that the letter specifies how to reach you for a possible interview. For example, "Please feel free to call me at your convenience to set up an interview so we can discuss my application and qualifications. You can reach me at 757-874-8989."

A cover letter should include your mailing address, the date, and the potential employer's mailing address. With the potential employer's mailing address, you should include the name and title of the person you are sending your letter and resume to if known. If you do not know the name but you do know the title, then just put the title. If you do not know the title but you do know the name, then just put the name. If you do not know the name or the title, you may put "Human Resources" or "To Whom It May Concern." It would be a good idea to make a phone call to the company and ask who you should send your resume to.

The next part of your letter is called the greeting. Never greet someone in a cover letter by their first name unless you are told to. For example, if the help-wanted ad says to send your resume to Sara, then your greeting would be "Dear Sara." However, if the help-wanted ad says to send your resume to Sara Jones, then your greeting would be "Dear Ms. Jones." Make sure that you use a colon at the end of the greeting instead of a comma. A colon is for business letters and a comma is for personal letters.

The body of your letter should only be two to four paragraphs. The first paragraph should start with something to grab the reader's attention. It should also state which job you are applying for and how you found out about the job. The next paragraph(s) should include relevant information about your qualifications and include a reference to your enclosed resume. Your final paragraph should give the reader your contact information and suggest what you would like for him/her to do (call you to set up an interview). You should always thank the reader for his/her time.

Close the letter with a formal closing,—such as "Sincerely," and leave some space to sign your name. You should also type your name and include an enclosure line for your resume.

Interviewing

The next step in the job search is to gain an interview. Hopefully your cover letter and resume did the job for you and the potential employer will call you to set up an interview. If you send out a cover letter and resume and do not hear from the potential employer within a reasonable amount of time, it is fine to call to make sure your resume/cover letter was received. Sometimes this helps to get your name heard, and you might just get that interview.

The goal of a cover letter and resume is to get you an interview. The goal of an interview is to get you the job (or at least another interview). Some companies will interview a potential employee several times before making a final decision. As long as you are invited back for another interview, you are still a candidate for the job.

Sample Cover Letter

Sandra Jenkins
901 Heron Drive
Newport News, VA 23602
January 15, 2008

James R. Smith
Director of Human Resources
Styons Agency
301 Jefferson Avenue
Newport News, VA 23601

Dear Mr. Smith:

Miriam Colon said, "Leadership is knowing what you want and making it happen." I know what I want and I am ready to make it happen. It is my desire to advance in the accounting field. I am responding to the advertisement you placed in *The Daily Press* on January 12, 2008, for an accounting supervisor. I believe I am the right person for that position.

As you can see from my enclosed resume, I have much experience in the accounting field. In my current position, I have worked diligently and have learned much. I am ready to put that knowledge into use at your company. I believe that there is no further room for me to advance in my current position.

Please feel free to call me at your convenience to set up a meeting so I can discuss my qualifications further. You can reach me at 757-874-8989. I look forward to hearing from you. Thank you for your consideration.

Sincerely,
(handwritten signature here)
Sandra Jenkins

Enclosure: Resume

In order to have a successful interview, here are several tips to keep in mind:

- Always arrive on time (a few minutes early is fine, but do not arrive too early)
- Dress appropriately
- Do not take your cell phone to the interview unless it is on silent and out of sight
- Do not bring any food or drink into the interview (including gum)
- Use your best manners with anyone you come into contact with
- Make eye contact with the interviewer
- Don't talk about your personal life
- Bring a copy of your resume
- Wait to be seated—do not sit down until you are told to have a seat or until the interviewer sits down
- Try not to fidget
- Don't wear too much perfume or cologne
- Don't wear too much makeup
- Never badmouth former employers
- Never bring up salary unless the interviewer brings it up first
- Use a firm handshake
- Keep a positive attitude
- Feel free to ask questions if you have them

- Answer questions thoroughly, but don't talk too much
- Listen carefully
- Use the name of the person who is interviewing you (Mr. or Mrs.)
- Always thank the interviewer for his/her time

In addition to the above tips, it is a good idea to prepare for some typical questions that may be asked. If you are currently employed elsewhere, you will most likely be asked why you are leaving that job. Be prepared to give an honest answer without talking badly about coworkers or your current boss. You can go to the Internet and search for interview questions that are currently popular to get an idea of what may be asked. Remember to be honest and thorough with your answers.

Follow Up

Very few jobs are actually offered during an interview. Usually the interviewer will inform you of the next step at the interview. For example, the interviewer may say that he/she will be in touch within two weeks. If you do not hear back from the interviewer or someone at the company, it is a good idea to follow up on the interview. You can call or send a letter to thank the person for the interview and express your continued interest in the position. If you don't hear anything in a reasonable amount of time, it is fine to call again. Remember, you can be persistent without making a pest of yourself.

Job Success

Once you have the job, continue to make a good impression so that you can keep your job and possibly advance. Make sure that you dress appropriately and are well groomed. Some companies have dress codes, and that will be conveyed to you upon starting the job. If there is no specific dress code, take notice of what others are wearing and dress similar to them. For example, if everyone is wearing a suit and tie, don't come in jeans and a T-shirt. Be on time for your job every day. Be courteous and gracious at all times. Be kind to others who work in the company even if they are not your boss. Listen carefully when going through training, and take good notes if necessary. Feel free to ask questions if you don't understand something. Be ready to help out wherever needed. Do not use company time or equipment for personal gain. Remember the Golden Rule!

Check Your Understanding

1. Is work a punishment from God? Why or why not?
2. List three characteristics of a lazy person that are written in Proverbs.
3. Give an example of a career line.
4. What is the difference between a job and a career?
5. What does an employment agency do?
6. List three items that should go on your resume and three items that should not.
7. What is a cover letter? Why is it important?

8. List three tips for a successful interview.
9. What is meant by following up after a job interview?
10. List three ways to have success on the job.

Reinforcement Assignments

1. Using the Internet or newspaper, find five help-wanted ads that interest you (jobs that you may be interested in when you are older and ready to begin your career). Bring in a copy of each ad and explain how you would respond to the ad if you wanted to apply for the job. Also, explain what you believe the qualifications would be for each job.

2. Write a cover letter for the help-wanted ad that follows. Assume that you have the education and experience necessary to apply for this position.

   US Newspaper, **Sunday, September 6, 2009:** Data Service Coordinator, Guidelines. An Internet-based nonprofit organization has an immediate need for an individual who has computer experience. This individual must be able to work well in a fast-paced environment. This individual must also be proficient in Word and Excel. Prior experience in the customer service and data entry field is a plus. Excellent communication skills are required. If interested, please send a cover letter and resume to: HR Director, Guidelines, 1212 Northgate Drive, Carrollton, VA 23314.

3. Create a resume of your current qualifications.
4. Create a resume of your future qualifications. This should include a college degree that you hope to attain and some work experience. This is for practice only. Remember to always be honest on resumes and never make up information.
5. Think of a job that you are interested in. Write a paragraph or two explaining what you think a typical day on the job would be like.
6. Critique the following job interview:

Interviewer: Hello, thanks for coming, have a seat.

Interviewee: Thank you. (Sits down)

Interviewer: Tell me about yourself.

Interviewee: I'm married and have two young children.

Interviewer: Why did you leave your previous job?

Interviewee: My previous employer accused me of doing things that I didn't do. He just didn't like me. I was so glad to get outta there! People were so mean and hateful. (Interviewee is chewing gum.)

Interviewer: Sorry to hear that. So, what can you offer this company?

Interviewee: I want to move up the corporate ladder right away. I don't enjoy menial work. How much does this job pay?

Interviewer: This job pays $15 per hour to start.

Interviewee: Okay, that will be fine for starters, but I do plan to move right up.

Interviewer: Well, I believe that just about covers it. Do you have any questions?

Interviewee: Nope.

Interviewer: Thanks for coming in, I'll be in touch.

Interviewee: Okay, see ya!

7. Create a list of questions that you think would be asked in a job interview for a sales clerk. What responses do you believe the interviewer would expect?

CHAPTER 2

DEBT

Introduction

Debt is something owed to another person or company where there is a sense of obligation to pay it back. Most people would like to stay out of debt, but in today's society it is not easy. Debt is not necessarily bad as long as it is handled properly. Most people cannot afford to buy a house without taking out a loan. Also, many people cannot afford to buy a car or pay for college without taking out a loan. This is not wrong if you can afford to make your payments and make them on time. The problem with debt is that many people choose to live on borrowed money and then end up in bankruptcy.

The Bible says that someone who borrows money and does not pay it back is wicked (Psalm 37:21), so make sure you are prepared to pay back whatever you borrow. Proverbs 22:7 says that the borrower will become a servant to the lender. For example, if you borrow money from someone, you will probably feel like you owe them something, in addition to the money, until you pay them back. There once was a family who got into a bind and had to borrow a lot of money from another family member. They were not able to pay back the loan for quite some time. Whenever the two families got together, the first family always felt like they had to do whatever the lending family requested of them.

Interest

Interest is the price you pay for using someone else's money. Most debt comes with interest. Debt can therefore be expensive because of the additional charges that interest brings. There are several different ways to calculate interest, but the simplest form is Principal x Rate x Time. Principal is the amount borrowed, rate is the interest rate expressed as a percentage, and time is based on years. For example, if you borrowed $2500 at 5% for 2 years, your interest would be $250 (2500 x 5% x 2).

Credit Cards

Some say that credit cards are bad. Actually, they can be if not used properly. However, most people need at least one credit card for booking hotel rooms, renting cars, etc. It is not a good idea to have a lot of credit cards, but one or two is fine. Many people get themselves into trouble by opening credit cards at every shopping location to get a discount on merchandise. Be very careful of this technique as it tends to make it too easy to overspend. Using credit cards can be expensive, addictive, and deceptive. Credit cards are expensive because of the interest. They are addictive because people often find it too easy to swipe their credit cards and pay later. They are deceptive because people tend to spend more money than they would have spent if they were using cash.

On the other hand, there are some good aspects of credit cards. They are great for emergencies. For example, if your car breaks down and you need a tow truck, your credit card may come in handy. They are also safer than cash because you can cancel them if they are lost or stolen, and you will not be held responsible for any charges beyond $50. Also, some places require a credit card to hold a reservation.

Using credit cards is fine as long as you pay them off every month. This way you will not have to pay interest. Make sure you pay them on time as well or you may incur additional fees. If you find that you used your card too much one month and cannot make the full payment, pay as much as you can by the due date and do not use your card again until it is paid in full! If you find that you cannot make your payment at all, contact your creditor immediately so they will know that you want to pay your bill and you are not just ignoring it. Usually they will work with you to straighten things out. This is not a situation you want to find yourself in. Be very careful when using credit cards!

In addition, be very careful to keep your credit card in a safe place, and never loan it to others. Always remember to get it back when you make a purchase. Be very aware of where your card is at all times. If it is lost or stolen, you want to report it immediately, and you cannot do that if you don't keep up with it.

Buying a Car

Buying a car can be one of the largest expenses you will ever have. If you want to purchase a new car, there is a good chance that you will have to finance it (make monthly payments). There are pros and cons to buying a new car versus a used car. Probably one of the most important aspects of buying a new car is the idea that you will not have to be concerned about prior misuse. On the other hand, if you buy a used car, sometimes you get a car that has not been properly maintained. Some car dealerships offer warranties on used cars as well as new cars. This will help alleviate the concerns that go along with buying a used car.

One of the major concerns of buying a new car is the cost. New cars cost much more than used cars. However, sometimes you can get a lower interest rate on a new car, so make sure you compare bottom lines (the total price you end up paying) when buying a car. In addition, do some research. There are many options available to consumers so that they can learn more about different cars.

If you must finance a car, make sure you understand the terms of the agreement. Some loans contain a balloon payment at the end of the loan. This is a final payment that can be quite expensive. Some people have to refinance their car at the end of the loan just to afford the balloon payment. Read the fine print on the loan agreement and ask important questions when financing a car. For example, a car was recently advertised on TV stating that the payments were only $129 per month; but if you read the fine print, it stated that a final payment of $3200 was due at the end of the loan.

In addition, if you finance a car it is wise to choose a short term. For example, if possible choose a three-year loan rather than a seven-year loan. Sure, the payments will be higher, but you can pay the car off faster than it depreciates (loses value), and you will save a lot of money in interest. You do not want to end up "upside down" with your car loan. This basically means that you owe more than your car is worth.

Another option is leasing a car. This also has pros and cons. Make sure you weigh all of your options. If you choose to lease, make sure you fully understand the lease agreement. These agreements often require large payments up front or at the end of the lease. In addition, you often are required to pay extra if you put more than the allotted miles on your car. This can be very expensive if you drive a lot. Remember that when you lease a car you do not really own it and you cannot make changes to the car (like adding a sunroof) without permission from the leaseholder.

The choice is yours, but if you want to be a wise consumer, you will do your research and read all agreements carefully.

Buying a Home

Buying a home is a huge decision, but it is usually well worth it. Most people will finance their home with a loan called a mortgage. A mortgage is a type of loan where the home goes to the lender if the buyer does not pay off the debt according to the terms of the loan. You can get a mortgage from a bank, mortgage company, or other lending institution. First-time homebuyers and low-income homebuyers can often qualify for government programs that offer better interest rates or certain tax incentives. Also, some people will qualify for VA (Veteran's Administration) loans, FHA (Federal Housing Authority) loans, and HUD (Housing and Urban Development) loans which may provide better interest rates.

Most mortgages have terms of either 15 or 30 years. Obviously, the 15-year loan will cost more per month, but in the long run you can save thousands of dollars in interest if you choose the 15-year loan. In addition, interest rates for 15-year loans are often slightly lower than 30-year rates.

You can get a fixed-rate mortgage or an adjustable-rate mortgage (ARM). With a fixed-rate mortgage, your interest rate does not change over the life of the loan. With an adjustable-rate mortgage, the interest rates can adjust up or down annually. However, to protect the borrower, most ARMs have a maximum rate of increase each year and a limit on the total maximum rate that can be charged. Be sure you understand the terms of the loan when taking out a mortgage. A fixed-rate mortgage is safer, but adjustable-rate mortgages can also work to your advantage. If you choose an adjustable-rate mortgage, make sure you know what the maximum amount you may have to pay will be. For example, on a $100,000 mortgage, a 1% increase is approximately $63 per month and a 5% increase is approximately $317 per month.

When you purchase a home, your payment will also include real estate taxes and homeowner's insurance. Both of these items will be discussed in later chapters, but be aware that you need to include these costs in your payment. Also, some homes are in neighborhoods that require you to pay association dues. In this case, you may want to include that amount in your payment as well. So your monthly payment will include principal, interest, real estate taxes, homeowner's insurance, and possibly other fees. Some loans also require mortgage insurance, which will be discussed later as well.

When shopping for a home, it is best to consult with a mortgage specialist before you begin shopping so you know how much you can afford. A mortgage specialist can work with you and help you determine the price range you should be considering. They can pre-qualify you to determine if you will be approved for your loan and how much of a loan you can take. Remember, you do not have to use the full amount that you qualify for. You should be comfortable with your monthly payment. You probably do not want to spend more than 25%-30% of your income on a house payment. Of course, this depends on other expenses that you have.

In addition to your monthly payment, there are other costs to consider when buying a home. First of all, most mortgages require a down payment. This can be substantial. For example, if you purchase a home for $150,000, the lender may require that you have 10% or $15,000 as a down payment, and then you get a mortgage for the remaining $135,000. Closing costs are also necessary when buying a home. In some cases, the seller will offer to pay part or all of your closing costs as an incentive to buying their home.

Closing costs consist of attorney's fees, recording costs, escrow accounts, points, and other processing fees. You will want to hire an attorney to be with you at closing to verify all documents and explain anything you do not understand. Recording costs are required by the city or county in which the home exists so that the deed (document that transfers ownership) can be recorded at the courthouse. Escrow accounts are basically holding accounts for taxes and insurance. Points are percentages of the loan—one point is equal to 1%. Points are paid as either loan origination fees or discount points. Loan origination fees are processing fees that are paid to the mortgage company for their work in securing the loan. Discount points may or may not be paid, but can be paid to buy down the interest rate. These closing costs can be financed in with the mortgage loan if necessary.

Financing College

College has become very expensive, and many people just cannot afford to pay the costs without some help. There are several ways to pay for college if you don't have the cash. You might be able to get a business to pay for your college if you promise to work for that company after graduation. You can also do a co-op, which means you go to school for a semester, then go to work for a semester to earn the money for school. The disadvantage to a co-op is that it takes longer, but the advantage is that you graduate without debt from student loans and you gain work experience.

Another way to pay for college is with scholarships and grants. The advantage is that you don't have to pay these back and you can go to school without taking time off to work. Sometimes these scholarships and grants will only work for full-time students. Many schools also offer a work-study program where you can go to school and work at the same time. Usually you work on campus and your hours will be based on your schedule so that you can get to all of your classes.

Many people choose to take out student loans to pay for college. This is one type of debt that is usually well worth it because the average college graduate makes much more money over a lifetime than someone who did not graduate from college. Most student loans do not require you to begin making payments until you have graduated from college and had time to begin working. If you choose to take out a student loan, weigh all of your options since there are many. Federal loan programs often offer lower interest rates than banks or other lending institutions.

Some people will find that they are eligible for federal or state aid. Sometimes this aid is in the form of a loan and sometimes it is in the form of a grant. To determine if you are eligible, you must fill out a form called the FAFSA (Free Application for Federal Student Aid). This is a fairly lengthy form with many questions that must be filed annually to continue aid. Most colleges have deadlines in February or March so be prepared to fill these forms out early.

Start researching your options early because it takes time to do this. Going to college is a wise decision, and anyone who wants to go should be able to find a way to pay for it.

Debt Consolidation

Some people end up in a lot of debt and need to consolidate their debt. This is done by taking out a larger loan to pay all of the smaller loans and spreading out the payments over a longer period of time. When this happens, some sort of collateral is usually required. In many cases, people can get a home-equity loan based on the equity in their home. Equity is the difference between what the home is worth and how much is owed on the home. The collateral in this case is the home. Be very careful when consolidating debt—you could lose your home!

Often when people consolidate debt they continue to overspend. This is the problem that got them in debt to begin with. If you choose to consolidate your debt you must also learn to stop overspending or you will find yourself in even more debt. In addition, you will find yourself paying for things long after they have served their purpose.

Check Your Understanding

1. What is debt?
2. What does the Bible say about someone who borrows money and does not pay it back?
3. What is interest?
4. Name two advantages to having a credit card.
5. What is a balloon payment?
6. Why should you choose a short-term loan rather than a long-term loan when financing a car?
7. What is a mortgage?
8. What is an ARM?
9. What does a monthly mortgage payment usually include?
10. Explain the difference between the two types of points.
11. What is a FAFSA?
12. What is debt consolidation? Why is it dangerous?

Reinforcement Assignments

1. Determine how much interest will be paid in the following situations using the simple interest formula.
   a. Principal = $3500, Rate = 4%, Time = 3 years
   b. Principal = $4500, Rate = 3%, Time = 4 years

    c.   Principal = $3750, Rate = 4%, Time = 6 months

    d.   Principal = $2800, Rate = 5%, Time = 9 months

2. Using the Internet, research vehicle leases. Type a one-page report discussing the advantages and disadvantages of leasing a vehicle.

3. Using the Internet or a newspaper, find three different lending institutions that offer mortgages. Compare the mortgage rates of each company including the fixed-rate and adjustable-rate mortgages.

4. Research a college or university and determine what type of work-study programs they have. Type a one- to two-page report on these programs.

5. If you earn $45,000 per year and do not want to spend more than 30% of your income on a house payment, what is the maximum monthly payment that you can afford?

CHAPTER 3

BUDGETING

Introduction

A budget is a plan for spending and saving money. Most budgets are done on a monthly basis. It is important to know where your money is going on a regular basis. Many people do not even realize how much they spend on many items until they begin budgeting.

Steps to Creating a Budget

The first step when creating a budget is to determine your monthly income from all sources including your job, alimony, child support, etc. In most cases it is easy to determine because the same amount is earned each month. In other cases, it is not as easy because the income may fluctuate. In these cases, you need to estimate the best you can. The next step is to determine the net income that you have available to spend each month. This is the amount after taxes and tithes. Most people have taxes taken out of their check every pay period, so that part is easy because it is already done for you. We will discuss this more in chapter 7.

No one is going to force you to tithe, but if you start tithing from the very beginning, it will be easier. A tithe is one-tenth. This means that 10% of your earnings, before taxes, should be given to your church. We should tithe because that is what God expects of us. It is the very least He has ever asked His people to give. You don't have to limit your giving to 10%; that should be a minimum. God promises that He will bless those who tithe. Read Malachi 3:10-12 to see what God says about tithing.

The third step when creating a budget is to identify where you expect your money to be spent and how much you will spend in each category. This can be tricky because many expenses are not exactly the same every month. Some categories you will use are rent/mortgage payment, utilities (gas and electric for your house), telephone, gas for your vehicles, car payments and any other loans you might have, food, clothing, medical, insurance, entertainment, and miscellaneous. Not everyone will have the same categories. Everyone should have a miscellaneous category because expenses always come up that don't necessarily fit into any other category. Also, it is very important to put some money into a savings account for the future and for unexpected expenses such as car repairs or medical bills that are not covered by insurance.

The next step is to calculate monthly averages for irregular items. This would possibly include insurance that is paid every six months or quarterly. It may include vacations and Christmas gifts. For example, if you pay your car insurance every six months and the cost is $1200, then your monthly amount would be $200 ($1200/6). You may want to put this money into your savings account or set up a separate checking account to store the money until you need to spend it.

Finally, add up all of your expenses and total them. If your expenses are more than your income, you need to make some adjustments until it evens out. The key is to end up with a zero balance. If your expenses are less than your income, put that money into your savings account for the future.

A Sample Budget

Suppose your gross pay (before taxes) is $4000 per month, and your net pay (after taxes) is $3500 per month.

Income	$3500
Tithes	400 (10% of $4000)
Rent	825
Food	350
Insurance	400

Utilities	150
Clothing	150
Medical	100
Gas for Car	175
Telephone	50
Entertainment	100
Miscellaneous	200
Car Payment	250
Savings	350

Groceries

Most high school students have no idea how much groceries cost. This is one expense that cannot be cut out of a budget. However, there are many ways to keep your food costs down. If you have the space available in your home, you can buy in bulk and usually save money. It is not always better to buy in bulk, so make sure you pay attention to unit costs. For example, if you buy a 52-ounce container of laundry detergent for $6.76, you are paying $.13 per ounce. If you buy a larger container, 168 ounces, and pay $22.68, you are actually paying $.135 per ounce which is not a better deal. Take your calculator with you so that you can compare prices. Also, use local store advertisements so you can compare sales.

Another way to save money on groceries is by using coupons. Some grocery stores will even double or triple your coupons and you can save even more. However, don't be tempted to buy something you don't need or really want just because you have a coupon.

Check Your Understanding

1. What is a budget?
2. List the steps to create a budget.
3. What is a tithe?
4. How are irregular items accounted for in a budget?
5. Name two ways to save on groceries.

Reinforcement Assignments

1. Which is the better buy: a 20-ounce coke for $1.20 or a six-pack of 16-ounce bottles for $5.28?
2. Which is the better buy: a 30-ounce bottle of dishwashing liquid for $2.10 or a 96-ounce bottle for $6.24?
3. Create a budget based on gross income of $3200 per month. Assume taxes are $480 per month.
4. If you plan to spend $2600 on a vacation next year, how would you account for that expense in your monthly budget?
5. Create a grocery budget and meal plan for one week for yourself. Make a list of everything you plan to eat for one week (do not eat out more than a time or two this week). Create a list of groceries and go to the grocery store or

shop online to price each item. Make sure you include the cost of the meals you eat out.

Project Hardship Budget

The idea is to create a budget for one month for a family in a hardship situation. No government assistance is allowed for this project because that would defeat the purpose of this assignment. Create a budget with documentation for the following situation:

Your annual income is $24,000 per year. Your spouse does not have any income. You have four children; ages are 8, 6, 3, and 1. Your 1-year-old is still in diapers. You have credit card debt of $175 per month. You have health insurance through your job, but it will cost you an additional $300 per month to add your family (optional).

The following items must be included in your budget: rent or mortgage expense, utilities, credit card debt, transportation, insurance, food, clothing, taxes, tithes, diapers, and miscellaneous. You must find an actual place to live and transportation. The other expenses can be estimated, but there needs to be some documentation of what your estimated cost will be. You can shop around for less expensive health insurance if you choose to. You may talk to your parents or other adults to get a good idea of what your cost will be for utilities and other such expenses. Your children will need some form of entertainment also, so make sure you provide that for them at whatever cost you can afford, and document. Assume an income tax rate of 7.65%. Create a 90-

meal (three meals a day for 30 days) plan with a grocery list. You may include telephone, cable, Internet, etc., in your budget, but you do not have to. Make sure you have some money set aside for savings.

CHAPTER 4

BANKING

Introduction

It is very important to know how to set up a checking account and a savings account. It is even more important to know how to keep accurate records and not rely on someone else to do it for you. Many students have debit cards and use them frequently. Debit cards are not necessarily a problem, but many young people do not keep accurate records of what they purchase with their debit cards and therefore do not keep accurate balances in their accounts. They just accept whatever the bank tells them they have in their accounts. This is not good financial management!

Choosing a Bank

There are many different banks and credit unions that would love to have you as a customer. When deciding on which bank you will use, be prepared to shop around. Some things to think about when choosing a bank are: location, services provided, fees charged, interest rates, and customer service. Most people like to use a bank that is fairly convenient to where they live or work. Decide what is important to you and compare several different banks and credit unions. Be aware that many credit unions will provide banking services to all types of people. Years ago, credit unions only served select groups of people (for example, people that worked for a particular company or industry). Some credit unions still do, but others will serve anyone. Remember, it never hurts to check out all of your options.

Checking Accounts

A checking account has many advantages. Often people choose to write checks instead of paying cash so they can have a record of money spent. Using checks instead of cash is a good way to budget your money. Also, it is safer than carrying around a large amount of cash. Today, many checking accounts come with debit cards or ATM cards so that cash is fairly easy to access. Be very careful to record all withdrawals and expenses when using either card. You do not want to overdraw (take out more money than you have in your account) your account because expensive penalties will likely be charged to you.

To open a checking account, you must go to your bank and sign a signature card and deposit some money to start your account. When using a checking account, make sure that you use the check register that comes along with your checks. This register is where you keep accurate records of deposits and withdrawals to/from your account. When writing a check make sure that you write legibly, and always sign your check the same way.

Many banks will charge a fee for having a checking account with them. However, some banks will waive that fee for students. Some banks charge a flat monthly fee no matter how many checks you write, and others charge a fee per check. Sometimes the bank will waive the fee as long as you keep a minimum balance in your account.

Some checking accounts offer automatic overdraft protection. This is a service that will cover you if you accidentally write a check for more than you have in your account (overdraft). If you have a savings account at the same bank, the money can be automatically transferred from your savings account to your checking account if an overdraft occurs. Another way to use automatic overdraft protection is through a credit card. In this case, your credit card is automatically charged for the overdraft and the money is transferred to your checking account. While this is a great idea, it should only be used in emergency situations. It should not be relied on regularly. If you have the option, choose the savings account instead of the credit card because it will keep you out of debt.

When overdrafts are charged to your credit card, interest begins accumulating immediately and often at a higher cash advance rate. This can lead to unmanageable debt if you are not careful. Also, many banks will only cover you through automatic overdraft protection a certain amount of times each month. If you rely on this, you may find yourself using it too much and therefore not getting the protection you expect.

ATMs are very convenient; sometimes a little too convenient. Often people take cash out when they really cannot afford to do so. Have you ever noticed that ATMs are often in shopping areas? They are in place so that you can feel free to shop impulsively. In addition, if the ATM you use is not your bank's ATM, you will likely be charged a service fee. If you choose to use an ATM, be very careful because of the risks involved. Always use an ATM that is located in a safe place because many people have been robbed at or near ATMs.

Bank Statements

When you set up a checking account, you will receive monthly bank statements from your bank. Pay very close attention to these statements and reconcile the statement with your checkbook register. Most of the time, your checkbook balance will not agree with the bank's balance. Usually the difference is due to timing issues. When you write a check, it takes some time to actually come out of your account unless the recipient of your check cashes it immediately. These checks that you have written and have not yet come through your bank are called outstanding checks.

The same is true with deposits. If you make a deposit on the last day of the month, it might not be included in your account until the next day; therefore it is called a deposit in transit. Typically, there are not many deposits that do not make it into your account immediately. In some cases, deposits are mailed to the bank and that can also be a reason for a deposit in transit.

Bank fees will show up on your bank statement, and you may not have already subtracted them from your checkbook balance. This is not a timing difference, but it is still an item that needs to be reconciled. Also, sometimes you or your bank will make errors when recording checks. This is another item that will need to be reconciled. The key is to reconcile the bank's balance with your checkbook balance.

A bank statement will look something like this:

Balance as of 1/1/09	$500
Deposits:	
1/2/09	$100
1/6/09	200
1/10/09	200
1/16/09	100
1/28/09	300
Total deposits	$900

Checks cleared:

#101	$50
#102	30
#103	20
#104	10
#106	20
#108	40
Total checks cleared	$170
Bank service charge	$15
Balance as of 1/31/09	$1215

Your checkbook balance will probably have a different balance, and you want to figure out why. For example, your checkbook may look like this:

Balance at 1/1/09	$500
Check #101	-50
Check #102	-30
Deposit 1/2/09	100
Check #103	-20
Deposit 1/6/09	200
Check #104	-10
Deposit 1/10/09	200
Check #105	-100
Check #106	-20
Deposit 1/16/09	100
Check #107	-20

Check #108	-40
Deposit 1/28/09	300
Check #109	-50
Check #110	-60
Deposit 1/31/09	500
Balance 1/31/09	$1500

In order to reconcile your bank statement, you must determine why there is a $285 difference between your checkbook balance at the end of the month and the ending balance on the bank statement. It doesn't really matter what you do first, but you will need to arrive at a new checkbook balance and a new bank balance that should equal. If you start with your checkbook, all you need to do is subtract any bank fees such as service charges that are listed on the bank statement but not in your checkbook. In this example, you will need to subtract the bank service charge of $15, which gives you a new checkbook balance of **$1485**.

Next, find the items listed in your checkbook that are not listed on the bank statement. The deposit your checkbook lists on 1/31/09 does not show up on the bank statement; therefore, it is a deposit in transit. It is a timing difference that must be accounted for in the bank reconciliation. So you would add $500 to your bank statement balance, which gives you a new balance of $1715. Then you would find any checks that are listed in your checkbook that are not listed on the bank statement. These outstanding checks, another timing difference, must be subtracted from your bank statement balance. Check #105 in the amount of $100 did not show up on the bank statement. Check #107 in the amount of $20, check #109 in the amount of $50, and check #110 in the amount of $60 did not show up on the bank statement. Therefore, you need to subtract each of these checks from your bank statement balance of $1715 to arrive at the reconciled balance of **$1485**. Now the two balances are equal and the bank statement and checkbook have been reconciled. The proper format for a bank reconciliation is:

Checkbook balance	**$1500**
Less: Bank service charge	-15
Corrected checkbook balance	**$1485**
Bank balance	**$1215**
Add: Deposits in transit	500
Subtotal	**$1715**
Less: Outstanding checks	
#105	$100
#107	20
#109	50
#110	60
Total	-230
Corrected bank balance	**$1485**

Savings Accounts

Savings accounts are pretty simple since there is not typically as much activity with savings accounts as with checking accounts. It is important that you ask any questions you may have when setting up a savings account because there may be certain rules that must be followed. For example, some banks will only pay interest if you keep a minimum balance in the account. Other banks will charge you a penalty for withdrawing too many times. Just be sure to understand all the rules. You should also keep a record of all deposits and withdrawals made to your account and compare it to your bank statement much like your checking account statement. The idea is to make regular deposits into the account and very few withdrawals, if any.

Check Your Understanding

1. What are some factors that you should consider when choosing a bank?
2. How do you open a checking account?
3. What is a check register used for?
4. What is automatic overdraft protection?
5. What is an outstanding check?
6. What is a deposit in transit?
7. What is the difference between a checking account and a savings account?

Reinforcement Assignments

1. Research three or four local banks or credit unions. Find out what services they offer, how many branches they have nearby, what fees they charge, and how long they have been in business. Make a chart comparing them.

2. Many banks and credit unions offer checkbook packets for high school students. These packets teach you how to write a check, how to make a deposit, and how to reconcile your bank statement. Call some local banks or credit unions to see if this is available to your school. If so, take advantage of this opportunity and also have someone from the bank come in and speak to your class.

3. Reconcile your checkbook with your bank statement given the following information:

Checkbook balance at 3/1/09	$100
Check #101	-30
Check #102	-25
Deposit 3/2/09	200
Check #103	-14
Deposit 3/5/09	150
Check #104	-80
Deposit 3/12/09	180
Check #105	-120
Check #106	-30
Deposit 3/17/09	468
Check #107	-28

Check #108	-35
Deposit 3/29/09	405
Check #109	-60
Check #110	-50
Deposit 3/31/09	200
Checkbook balance 3/31/09	**$1231**

Bank statement balance 3/1/09	**$100**
Deposits	
3/2/09	$200
3/6/09	150
3/12/09	180
3/18/09	468
3/29/09	405
Total deposits	$1403
Checks cleared	
#101	$30
#102	25
#104	80
#105	120
#107	28
#108	-35
Total checks	$318
Bank service charge	$10
Balance as of 3/31/09	**$1175**

CHAPTER 5

INVESTING

Introduction

Now that you have learned a little about making money, budgeting money, and staying out of debt, let's talk about putting your money to work for you. Investing is a way of saving money with the hopes of increasing it. The purpose of investing is to increase your assets (things you own). There are many reasons to increase your assets such as retirement, a new home, college educations for your children, and money to use if you are temporarily out of work.

Read Matthew 25:14-30. The parable of the talents teaches us to be wise with what we are given. We should be wise with our money by investing it to make it grow.

However, we need to be very careful not to waste it on unwise investments. Have you ever heard of a get-rich-quick scheme? Usually these are not wise investments. The next time you see such an advertisement on television, read the fine print at the bottom of your screen. The fine print usually says "Results not typical." If an investment opportunity sounds too good to be true, it probably is!

Investing Guidelines

There are many ways to invest your money. In this book we will only cover a few basic ways. However, some guidelines will work with any investment. First of all, make sure you understand exactly what you are getting into. Often there are strict penalties for removing money from your investments. Some investments will also offer tax benefits, but these are the ones that will charge penalties and additional taxes if you take the money out too soon.

All investments carry some sort of risk. Make sure you understand the risks and evaluate these risks to determine if this investment is too risky or not. Typically the higher the risk, the higher the rate of return (what you can expect to get out of the investment). For example, don't put a lot of money in a very risky investment if you cannot afford to lose it.

Make sure to seek diversity in your investing. Don't invest everything you have in one area because if that investment fails, you have nothing to fall back on. That is, don't invest all of your money in a particular industry because you never know what may happen. Real estate is typically a good investment, but in recent years there have been many problems in this area. The bottom line is to research any potential investments thoroughly before making the final decision to invest.

Low-Risk Investments

Some investments are virtually risk-free. United States savings bonds, savings accounts, and certificates of deposit are among those investments that do not carry much risk. However, these investments do not offer a high rate of return either. It is a good idea to have some money in these types of investments because they are fairly safe. Talk to your local bank representative for more information on these investments so that you can get up-to-date interest rates.

Retirement Plans

Most high school students are not thinking about retirement at this point. However, the sooner you start saving for retirement the better. When you begin working, your employer may offer a retirement plan. It is usually a good idea to take full advantage of such plans. As with any other investment, make sure you understand what you are getting into. Many employers will offer a 401(k) plan, which is a retirement plan that is tax-deferred. This means that you do not pay taxes on that money until you take it out of the account (hopefully when you retire).

This plan allows you to have a percentage of your gross pay taken out of your check before you actually get the check. This money goes into your retirement plan. Your employer may also make contributions to your account either through matching or profit sharing.

There are many other types of retirement plans, but the 401(k) is one of the most common types. Some larger companies have their own plans. These plans vary by employer. Whatever the case, seriously consider taking part in your employer's plan. The sooner you start, the more money you will have when you are ready to retire.

Stocks and Bonds

The main difference between stocks and bonds is that stocks represent ownership and bonds represent loans. Stocks are also more risky than bonds. When you buy stock in a corporation, you actually own a percentage of that corporation. When you buy corporate bonds, the corporation owes you money but you do not have ownership in that company.

The basic function of the stock market is to provide funds for corporations. These corporations raise money by selling stock to investors. Some corporations are private and some are public. The private corporation will not offer its stock for sale to the general public. A public corporation will offer its stock to the general public. To purchase stock, you can obtain the help of a stockbroker or you can buy online through an online broker.

You will pay a fee for your transactions. You will usually pay more to a stockbroker than online, but the stockbroker can give you good advice.

It is important to remember that stocks will increase and decrease in value. When looking to invest in stocks, consider the long-term trend. Stocks fluctuate on a daily basis. When stock prices are going up it is called a bull market, and when prices are going down it is called a bear market. Chances are that stocks will go down for certain periods of time and then back up for certain periods of time. Be patient when investing in stocks.

Investors earn money in the stock market by selling their stock at a higher price than it was purchased for (capital gain) and by earning dividends. A dividend is money paid to stockholders by the corporation. Dividends are not guaranteed but are usually paid when the company is doing well. Dividends are paid per share and are usually paid quarterly or annually. For example, if you owned 10 shares of Company A and a dividend of .50 per share was issued, you would receive $5.

You can track stocks online at several sites. One site is the New York Stock Exchange (NYSE.com). If a company trades on the New York Stock Exchange, you can find out the current value of the stock at any time. There are other stock exchanges as well, but the New York Stock Exchange is the largest. Many well-known corporations trade their stock on this exchange.

The Securities and Exchange Commission (SEC) is a federal agency that keeps watch over the stock market. It exists to enforce the laws that pertain to the stock market and other investments. This agency can also help you understand the stock market and other types of investments better. It has information about fraudulent investments that can be very helpful. Go to their website to find a lot of useful information about investing: www.sec.gov.

Compound Interest

In chapter 2 we discussed interest—the price you pay for using someone else's money. In this section we will discuss the benefits of interest. When investing, interest can be earned instead of paid. In other words, we are now talking about your money and someone else paying you to use it. When you invest your money into a savings account or some other interest-bearing account, you earn interest on your money. Even better, your interest will earn interest on your money too. This is called compound interest. Interest can compound at different intervals, such as yearly, monthly, quarterly, or even daily. This means that the interest is added to your original principal yearly, monthly, quarterly, etc.

For example, suppose you deposited $100 into an account that earns 7% interest and compounds annually. At the end of two years, you would have $114.49 in your account. This is calculated as follows:

$100 x 0.07 = $7 interest earned the first year. Then you add the $7 to the original $100 and have $107. For the second year, you take the new principal of $107 x 0.07 = $7.49. Add the $7.49 to the $107 and you end up with $114.49 at the end of year two.

The formula for calculating compound interest is Principal (1 + rate of interest) squared for two years, cubed for three years, etc. This may not seem all that great, but consider a larger investment for a longer period of time and it seems pretty good! For example, $1000 invested into an account that earns 7% interest would net you $1967 in 10 years if compounded annually.

Check Your Understanding

1. What is rate of return?
2. Typically, if an investment is very risky, is the rate of return higher or lower?
3. Why should you seek diversity when investing?
4. Give an example of a low-risk investment.
5. When do you pay taxes on the money you invest in a 401(k) plan?
6. What is the main difference between stocks and bonds?
7. What is the basic function of the stock market?
8. What is the difference between a private corporation and a public corporation?
9. What is a capital gain?
10. What is a dividend?

Reinforcement Assignments

1. How much would you have at the end of five years if you invested $500 into an account that pays you 5% interest compounded annually?

2. If you own 100 shares of stock of a company and that company declares dividends of .25 per share, how much would you earn in dividends?

3. If you purchased 300 shares of stock of a certain company for $15 per share and then sold all 300 shares for $18 per share, what would be your capital gain?

4. Research *insider trading* and write a paragraph on what it is and why it is illegal.

Stock Market Project

Choose a company that sells its stock publicly and can be found on the NYSE. Do some research on that company and prepare a one-page report on it. Include in your paper the following information:

- General information about the company and its products or services
- Ticker symbol
- Total dividends paid last year

At least three of the following: earnings per share last year, number of shareholders of record at the last year end, number of shares outstanding at the last year end, any information on stock splits, when the next dividends are due to be paid, when the company went public (when it first sold stock to the general public), when the company began, information on how the company began, any information from outside sources that rate the company's performance.

Prepare a poster that includes the following information:

- Company name
- Ticker symbol
- Graph of stock prices for a three-week period with at least six different dates recorded
- Any other pictures or information about the company including trademarks or other symbols

Present the poster to your class and have each classmate do the same; then vote on which stock would be the best to invest in.

CHAPTER 6

INSURANCE

Introduction

Insurance protects us from the financial loss of things that we value. Insurance is classified as a transfer of risks. Most anything can be insured if you are willing to pay the price for the insurance. In this chapter we will discuss health insurance, life insurance, car insurance, homeowner's insurance, and disability insurance. Some types of insurance are required by law and others are not. An insurance agent can help you determine how much coverage you need and how much it will cost. The money you pay for your insurance is called a premium. The premium is determined based on a number of factors such as the cost of the item to be insured and the risk involved. For example, your car insurance premium will be higher if you drive an expensive car (cost of item insured) and have had a lot of accidents or speeding tickets (risk involved).

Your insurance will pay for certain bills that you incur so that it doesn't come out of your pocket. However, many insurance policies have a deductible attached. This is the amount you pay out of pocket for each incident. For example, if you have health insurance and you spend several days in the hospital, your insurance would pay those fees for you minus the deductible that you pay. A day or two in the hospital can cost thousands of dollars, so health insurance is important to have.

When shopping for insurance, it is important to compare apples to apples. Make sure you understand exactly what your coverage is and what the limitations are. Also make sure you understand deductibles. Find an insurance agent who is willing to spend time with you and go over all the information on your policy, helping you to understand anything that is confusing. It is wise to be careful not to over-insure or under-insure. If you over-insure you are wasting money, and if you under-insure you are setting yourself up for a financial disaster.

Car Insurance

Car insurance is required by law. Each state has its own guidelines for how much insurance must be carried. Furthermore, if you finance your car, your lender will also require car insurance. It is wise to have more than the state minimums if you have positive net worth (your assets are higher than your liabilities). Your objective with car insurance is to adequately protect your assets without wasting money on unnecessary premiums.

There are different types of car insurance, and each type covers something different. All of these components are added together into one policy. One component is called bodily injury. This covers injury or death caused by you as a driver and resulting from a car accident that was your fault. This covers people in other cars, pedestrians, passengers in the car you are driving, and you and your family while driving someone else's car including rental cars. Usually there are two amounts for bodily injury coverage; one amount is the maximum amount your insurance will pay if you injure or kill one person and the other amount is the maximum amount your insurance will pay per accident if you injure or kill more than one person (no matter how many people were involved).

Another component of car insurance is property damage. This covers damage you cause to other people's property, including their car. For example, if you back into someone else's car and damage that car, this is the part of your car insurance that pays for that. Also, if you run into someone's mailbox this covers you.

A third component of car insurance is collision. This covers damages to your car when you collide with another vehicle or another object. So if you back into someone else's car and damage that car and your car, your collision component will pay for the damage done to your car.

Another component of car insurance is comprehensive. This covers loss or damage done to your car that was not caused by a collision. Theft, fire, and vandalism are covered here.

Most car insurance policies have deductibles that you must pay out of your pocket. For example, you may have a $100 deductible on comprehensive and a $200 deductible on collision. Therefore, if your car is vandalized and it will cost $300 to repair it, you must pay the first $100 and insurance will pay the rest up to your maximum. If you run into someone's mailbox and cause $150 worth of damage to your car, you must pay for that out of your own pocket because it is below your deductible of $200.

Homeowner's Insurance

There are four basic types of homeowner's insurance: property damage, liability, mortgage, and title. Property damage insurance is required by mortgage lenders. This covers damage to the home from fires, storms, etc. It does not cover normal repairs or termite damage in most cases. Some policies cover floods and others do not. As with any insurance, make sure you know what is covered and what isn't. You will also probably have a deductible for this.

You can add your furnishings and personal injury and relocation expenses as well. Covering your furnishings is important because that could really add up if you had to buy all new furniture. You can also choose to cover personal belongings such as clothes and jewelry. Personal injury may or may not be necessary depending on your health insurance policy. Relocation expense coverage is a nice option to help cover the costs of living elsewhere while your home is being repaired. For example, if your house caught on fire and a large portion of your home was damaged, you would need a place to live while your home was being repaired. Relocation expense coverage would pay for that place to live.

Liability insurance covers other people who get injured on your property. For example, if someone was in your yard and fell and broke a bone, this would cover the cost of that person's medical bills. This is important to have because cases abound where people have been sued for thousands of dollars to cover such expenses.

Mortgage insurance pays off the remaining mortgage if the insured dies. It declines as the mortgage balance declines. This is much like a life insurance policy, which will be discussed later in this chapter.

Title insurance pays to defend your right of ownership to the property if you must go to court. Many mortgage lenders require this coverage.

Another type of insurance that is similar to homeowner's insurance is renter's insurance. This insurance covers your furnishings and other belongings when you are renting property. This type of insurance is relatively inexpensive and is definitely worth having.

Life Insurance

Life insurance is purchased to protect your loved ones financially after your death. It can be used for funeral expenses as well as lost income. Some employers offer life insurance as a benefit, but usually it is not enough and you lose it when you change jobs. Therefore, it is wise to purchase another policy. There are two main types of life insurance: term and whole-life.

Term insurance is purchased for a set period of time, and at the end of the time the policy must be renewed if you intend to stay covered. When renewing term insurance, the cost goes up. Sometimes people choose term life insurance instead of mortgage insurance. It is a good idea to compare prices and coverage options on each to see which one works best for you.

Whole-life insurance is typically more expensive than term, but it creates a cash reserve. It does not expire like term insurance does. It covers you for your entire life; it does not increase with age.

To determine how much life insurance a person needs, many variables within each family must be considered. These variables include a person's income and expenses. An insurance agent can help you determine how much insurance you need.

Disability Insurance

Disability insurance is often overlooked. This insurance will cover your expenses if you cannot work due to illness or injury. Some employers offer this type of insurance. One type of disability insurance is called workers' compensation. This only covers workers who are injured or have an illness due to their job. Employers pay for this insurance.

There are short-term and long-term disability policies. Short-term policies only cover you for a short period of time and long-term policies can cover you until you reach retirement age. These policies will only cover a portion of your lost income, not the entire amount. Again, just make sure you fully understand your coverage so you can be prepared.

Health Insurance

Often employers offer health insurance as an employee benefit. Some employers pay the entire premium and some pay partial premiums. Employees usually need to pay for additional coverage for family members. Health insurance is expensive, so if your employer will provide it, that is a great benefit. Health insurance covers expenses such as doctor's visits, routine tests, emergency room visits, lab procedures, prescriptions, hospitalizations, surgeries, stitches, casts, and sometimes even dental work and eye care.

Many employers offer health insurance through a health maintenance organization (HMO) because it is less expensive. When covered under an HMO, the insured usually pays a copayment with each doctor's visit. This amount varies, but it is usually between $20 and $50 per visit. The insurance pays the rest. Also, when using an HMO, the insured must use a doctor within the network. The network is a group of doctors who agree to certain terms of the HMO and join the organization. The insured must choose a primary care physician within the organization and then get his or her approval before seeing a specialist. Even though there are drawbacks to using an HMO, the benefits usually outweigh them.

Check Your Understanding

1. What is a premium?
2. What is a deductible?
3. What does bodily injury cover under car insurance?
4. What does car insurance/property damage cover?
5. What is the difference between collision and comprehensive car insurance?
6. Which type of homeowner's insurance would cover the cost to repair your home if it had a fire?
7. What is mortgage insurance?
8. What is the difference between term life insurance and whole-life insurance?
9. What does workers' compensation cover?
10. What are some expenses usually covered by health insurance?
11. What is an HMO?

Reinforcement Assignments

1. Assume two people were in an accident and ended up with the exact same injuries. If neither had health insurance, the total cost for each would be as follows:
    -   $5678 for the hospital stay
    -   $345 for the emergency room visit
    -   $200 for the follow-up visit to the doctor
    -   $160 in prescriptions

        Calculate how much each person would pay based on their health insurance if one had an HMO and the other had a health insurance plan that was not an HMO.

        HMO plan: No deductible, $100 copayment per hospital stay, $45 copayment for the emergency room visit, $25 copayment for the doctor's visit, $10 copayment for the prescription.

        Other health insurance plan: $200 annual deductible, 20% coinsurance (the amount you pay for each fee after meeting your deductible) for all hospital stays, doctors' visits, emergency room visits, and prescriptions.

2. If your car insurance has $10,000 in collision coverage and you run into another car causing $6500 worth of damage, how much will your insurance pay to repair the car if your deductible is $500?

3. Contact a life insurance agent in your area and ask him/her to show you how to determine which life insurance policy is best for you and how much it will cost. Be sure to explain to the agent that this is for a class assignment.

CHAPTER 7

TAXES AND WAGES

Introduction

There are many types of taxes that must be paid. Most places charge a sales tax for each item purchased. This amount varies based on the locality where it is charged. For example, if you purchase an item that costs $20, and the sales tax rate is 5%, you would pay $1 in sales tax. This tax is collected at the time of purchase and the business then pays this tax to the state or locality where it is due.

In this chapter we will discuss payroll taxes, income taxes, real estate taxes, and personal property taxes. These taxes are used to pay for a wide variety of government programs and services such as libraries, schools, roads, police departments, etc. It is important to pay your taxes so these programs can run efficiently. Paying taxes is not an option; it is a responsibility. Jesus even spoke of paying taxes in the Bible. In Matthew 22:21, He said that we should give to Caesar what is Caesar's and to God what is God's.

Wages and Payroll Taxes

Before we can discuss payroll taxes, it is important to understand payroll. When you have a job, you get a paycheck for the job that you perform. You may get paid a salary or an hourly wage or a commission. If you are paid a salary, you will get the same amount each paycheck. For example, if your salary is $500 per week, then your total earnings before any deductions would be $500 each week. If you are paid an hourly wage, you will multiply your hourly rate by the number of hours worked per pay period to get your gross pay. Gross pay is the amount you earn before any taxes or other deductions are taken out. For example, if you work 40 hours per week and your hourly rate is $10, you will earn $400 per week before deductions. If you are paid a commission, you are paid based on how much you sell or produce. For example, if you receive 10% of every sale you make and you sold $3000 worth of products, your gross pay would be $300. Some jobs pay a salary or hourly wage plus commission.

Most businesses must pay overtime wages to hourly wage earners who work more than 40 hours in a week. This is one and a half times the regular pay rate. For example, if your pay rate is

$12 per hour and you worked 42 hours in a week, then the first 40 hours would be calculated based on regular pay of $12 and the other two hours (overtime) would be calculated based on $18 per hour (1½ x 12). Therefore, the gross pay for this week would be $516, calculated as follows: 40 x 12 = 480, 18 x 2 = 36, then add 480 and 36 which is equal to 516. Net pay is the amount of your paycheck after all taxes and other deductions are taken out of gross pay.

Payroll taxes are the taxes deducted from our paychecks. These taxes include Social Security, Medicare, federal, state, and local taxes. Social Security and Medicare taxes are deducted from each paycheck at the same rate. For 2012, the rate was 4.2% for Social Security and 1.45% for Medicare. You can go to www.irs. gov to get updated rates. Federal and state taxes are based on how much you earn, whether or not you are married, and how many exemptions you have.

When you first begin a job, you will be required to fill out a W-4 form. This form is used to determine how much to deduct from your paycheck for federal and state taxes. For example, if you are single and live with your parents, then you have no exemptions so you file single—0. The company you work for will use a chart or computer program to determine how much to deduct for your taxes. If you will only be working part-time and do not expect to make very much money, you may file exempt and no federal or state taxes will be deducted from your check. Be very careful, though, because you may end up owing taxes at the end of the year. Local taxes vary by locality, and many places do not even have these taxes.

At the end of the year, you will receive a W-2 form, which lists the total of all wages you earned from a particular company and a total of all taxes withheld from your paychecks over the year. You should receive this form in the mail around the end of January for the preceding year. This form is necessary when filing your income taxes. You must attach a copy of this form to your federal and state tax returns. You will also receive a copy to keep for your records. If you had more than one job, you will receive a separate W-2 for each company you worked for.

Income Taxes

The payroll taxes deducted from your paycheck are used to pay your income taxes. These taxes are filed once per year. The federal tax form is due April 15, and the state tax form varies based on the state you live in. You will file a 1040 for federal taxes. This form has shorter versions also. There are many schedules that go along with your 1040 depending on your income and expenses. Schedule A and B are two forms that many people use, and we will discuss those.

Schedule A is for itemized deductions. Itemized deductions are allowable deductions from your income. These deductions can help lower your taxes. Certain items such as mortgage interest, personal property taxes, real estate taxes, state taxes, and charitable contributions are deductible. You can find a copy of Schedule A at the IRS website. Every taxpayer is allowed a standard deduction that is determined by the IRS, but if you have more itemized deductions than the standard deduction, you may file Schedule A and save some money.

Schedule B is simply a listing of interest and dividends. This form is also available at the IRS website. This form is used to report where your earned interest and dividends came from. You can find a copy of Schedule B at the IRS website. The instructions to these schedules are also available on this website.

Real Estate Taxes

Real estate taxes are paid on your home and land that you own. These taxes vary by locality. Many people pay their real estate taxes with their mortgage payment. This money goes into an escrow account that holds the money until the taxes are due and then pays the taxes to the locality where they are due. This tax is calculated based on your home's value as decided by city or county assessors. For example, if you purchased a home for $100,000 and 10 years later the city assessed your home at $150,000, you will be taxed based on the $150,000. If your tax rate is 1%, then your taxes will be $1500.

Personal Property Taxes

Personal property taxes are paid on certain things you own. Some items that personal property taxes are paid on are cars, trucks, motorcycles, boats, jet skis, etc. These taxes are also paid to your local government, and the rates vary by locality. These taxes are usually paid either once or twice a year depending on the locality where these items are stored. The tax is based on the value of the property determined by city or county assessors. For example, if you own a car that you paid $14,000 for and the assessors valued the car at $12,000, then you would be taxed on the $12,000. If your tax rate is 3%, then you would pay $360 per year.

Check Your Understanding
1. What does the government use our tax money for?
2. Explain the difference between a salary, a commission, and an hourly wage.
3. What is gross pay?
4. What is net pay?
5. When is the federal income tax form due?
6. What are itemized deductions?
7. What are real estate taxes?
8. What are personal property taxes?

Reinforcement Assignments
1. If you purchased an item that cost $40, and the sales tax rate is 4%, how much sales tax would you pay?
2. If you purchased an item that cost $200, and the sales tax rate is 5%, how much sales tax would you pay?
3. What is gross pay for someone who worked 40 hours in one week at an hourly wage of $12?

4. What is gross pay for someone who worked 42 hours in one week at an hourly wage of $12? (Don't forget overtime.)

5. Go to the IRS website, www.irs.gov, and print out a copy of form W-4. Fill out this form for yourself.

6. If you purchased a home for $125,000, and 15 years later the city assessed your home's value to be $275,000, how much would you pay in annual real estate taxes if the tax rate is 1.5%?

7. If you purchased a car for $35,000, and four years later the city assessed the car's value to be $12,000, how much would you pay in annual personal property taxes if the tax rate is 3.5%?

CHAPTER 8

PERSONAL FINANCIAL STATEMENTS

Introduction

Personal financial statements help you determine if you have positive or negative net worth. Net worth is equal to assets minus liabilities. If assets are greater than liabilities, you have positive net worth. If liabilities are greater than assets, you have negative net worth. Assets are items you own, and liabilities are what you owe. For example, if you own a car that is worth $10,000 and you owe $4000 on it, your net worth in the car is $6000.

It is a good idea to prepare personal financial statements annually. The goal should be to increase your net worth. Some people have negative net worth, especially when first starting out. The key is to recognize it and work toward fixing it.

Assets

Some examples of assets are cars, houses, money, stocks, bonds, retirement accounts, and other investments. The difficult part of counting your assets is that you must use current values and not original costs. Sometimes it is difficult to determine current values. The current value should be what you could sell that asset for. There are many ways to get current values. For example, a house can be appraised by a real estate appraiser. The value of cars can be determined through car dealers and auto publications. Some items may need to be estimated because it is difficult or expensive to get an appraisal. You will not include items of sentimental value (like photo albums) because they have little worth to someone else.

Liabilities

Some examples of liabilities are mortgages, loans payable, and balances carried on your credit cards (hopefully you pay them off every month and do not carry a balance). Liabilities are easier to calculate since you just use the current amount due. Just call the creditor and ask for a payoff amount to get an accurate amount due.

Net Worth

Once you have determined the value of your assets and the value of your liabilities, you simply subtract total liabilities from total assets to arrive at net worth. This number is useful for many other financial decisions. For example, in chapter 6 we discussed using your net worth to determine how much insurance to purchase. Your net worth is also helpful when requesting a loan. Therefore, keep good records of your assets and your liabilities so that you can easily prepare a personal financial statement.

Personal Financial Statement Example

Assets

House	$250,000
Cash in savings	35,000
Cash in checking	7,000
Stocks	28,000
401(k) plan	90,000
Cars	28,000
Miscellaneous*	12,000
Total assets	$450,000

Liabilities

Mortgage	$185,000
Car loans	8,000
Student loans	20,000
Total liabilities	$213,000
Net worth	$237,000

*Includes furniture, electronics, jewelry, clothing

Check Your Understanding

1. What is an asset? What is a liability?
2. If assets are greater than liabilities, do you have positive or negative net worth?
3. What should you do if you have negative net worth?
4. Give two examples of assets.
5. Give two examples of liabilities.
6. Should you use current values or original costs when calculating assets?
7. Name two ways to determine current values of assets.
8. Why shouldn't you include items that have sentimental value in your financial statements?
9. How do you determine net worth?

Reinforcement Assignments

1. Given the following information, what are your total assets?
   - Current appraised value of house: $480,000
   - Current value of cars: $24,000
   - Cash in savings: $16,000
   - Cash in checking: $4,500
   - Current value of 401(k) plan: $260,000
   - Current value of miscellaneous items: $19,000
2. Given the following information, what are your total liabilities?

- Mortgage: $350,000
- Car loans: $18,000
- Student loans: $12,000

Prepare a personal financial statement using the information in #1 and #2 above.

CONCLUSION

As you can see, there is much to learn about personal finance. The sooner you start, the better! Keeping good control over your finances is not always easy. However, being aware of these basic financial concepts will give you a head start as you begin your life as an adult.

One lesson I hope you will take away from this book is to be a good steward of your money and material possessions. Remember to put God first in your life and trust Him to guide you in the right direction. There are many other verses in the Bible about money and material possessions. Take the time to read these verses and learn even more about God's plan for your finances.

ACKNOWLEDGMENTS

I want to thank my husband Bryan, my son Shayne, and my daughter Krysten for all of their support and understanding. I couldn't have done this without you. I would also like to thank my other family members for their support and encouragement.

I certainly would have never thought to write this book if it hadn't been for all of my Christian Finance students. I have truly enjoyed teaching all of you! Most importantly, I would like to thank my Lord and Savior Jesus Christ, because I can do all things through Him who gives me strength!

ABOUT THE AUTHOR

Christian Finance for Teens is Cindy Kersey's first book. She was born and raised in Hopewell, VA, attended Longwood College, and graduated with a degree in Business Administration with a concentration in Accounting. She worked in the accounting field for many years, which included owning her own small accounting business. Her family has always been extremely important to her, so she worked from home while her children were young. For the past ten years she has taught bible and business classes at Hampton Christian High School in Hampton, VA, where her children attended. This book was inspired by her one-semester course on Christian Finance taught at Hampton Christian.

Printed in the USA
CPSIA information can be obtained
at www.ICGtesting.com
JSHW080004150824
68134JS00021B/2279